TIME FOR KIDS
BOOK OF WHY
REALLY COOL PEOPLE & PLACES

TIME For Kids

Managing Editor: Nellie Gonzalez Cutler
Editor: Brenda Iasevoli
Creative Director: Jennifer Kraemer-Smith

Time Home Entertainment

Publisher: Jim Childs
Vice President, Brand & Digital Strategy: Steven Sandonato
Executive Director, Marketing Services: Carol Pittard
Executive Director, Retail & Special Sales: Tom Mifsud
Executive Publishing Director: Joy Bomba
Director, Bookazine Development & Marketing: Laura Adam
Vice President, Finance Director: Vandana Patel
Publishing Director: Megan Pearlman
Assistant General Counsel: Simone Procas
Assistant Director, Special Sales: Ilene Schreider
Brand Manager: Jonathan White
Associate Prepress Manager: Alex Voznesenskiy
Associate Production Manager: Kimberly Marshall
Associate Project Manager: Stephanie Braga

Editorial Director: Stephen Koepp
Senior Editor: Roe D'Angelo
Copy Chief: Rina Bander
Design Manager: Anne-Michelle Gallero
Editorial Operations: Gina Scauzillo

Special thanks: Katherine Barnet, Brad Beatson, Jeremy Biloon, Susan Chodakiewicz, Rose Cirrincione, Assu Etsubneh, Mariana Evans, Christine Font, Susan Hettleman, Hillary Hirsch, David Kahn, Amy Mangus, Nina Mistry, Dave Rozzelle, Ricardo Santiago, Adriana Tierno

Contents of this book previously appeared in Time For Kids Big Book of WHY.

For information on TIME FOR KIDS magazine for the classroom or home, go to TIMEFORKIDS.COM or call 1-800-777-8600.
For subscriptions to SI KIDS, go to SIKIDS.COM or call 1-800-889-6007.

Published by TIME FOR KIDS Books,
An imprint of Time Home Entertainment Inc.
135 West 50th Street
New York, NY 10020

ISBN 10: 1-60320-984-0
ISBN 13: 978-1-60320-984-7

We welcome your comments and suggestions about TIME FOR KIDS Books. Please write to us at:
TIME FOR KIDS Books, Attention: Book Editors,
P.O. Box 11016, Des Moines, IA 50336-1016
If you would like to order any of our hardcover Collector's Edition books, please call us at1-800-327-6388 (Monday through Friday, 7 a.m. to 8 p.m., or Saturday, 7 a.m. to 6 p.m., Central Time).

1 QGT 14

Picture credits
t = top, b = bottom, c = center, r = right, l = left

Front and Back cover:
The Statue of Liberty: Joshua Haviv, shutterstock.com
Pyramids, Cairo/Giza, Egypt: WitR, shutterstock.com
Gold Crown with Jewels: Ivan Ponomarev, shutterstock.com
Leaning Tower of Pisa: Lukiyanova Natalia / frenta, shutterstock.com
Eiffel Tower: Nerthuz, shutterstock.com
Abraham Lincoln: ra3rn, shutterstock.com
Australia: AridOcean, shutterstock.com
The Colosseum in Rome: abadesign, shutterstock.com
Viking: 83540536, Bob Carey, gettyimages.com

Contents Page:
Soren Pilman/Istockphoto, T-Design/Shutterstock, Library of Congress Prints and Photographs Division, Washington, D.C., Bryan Busovicki/Shutterstock

Inside:
USMC via National Archives: 24t, 25t.
Architect of the Capitol: 33r.
Bigstock: Enrico Beccari: 4l, 17t, 21t.
Dreamstime: Xdrew: 35t, Fabien Rigollier: 39, Bstefanov: 43b, Tupungato: 44t.
Fotolia: Miklav: 9b, Photlook: 29b.
Getty Images: Hulton Archive/Archive Photos: 45b, Apic/Hulton Archive: 11l, Hulton Archive: 11r, FPG/Archive Photo: 22t.
Istockphoto: Jan Rihak: 36, 48, Luoman: 42b, Janne Ahvo: 4r, 13t, Hulton Archive: 15, Soren Pilman: 22b.
Kurpfälzisches Museum: Gerard van Honthorst: 44b.
Library of Congress Prints and Photographs Division, Washington, D.C.: 8t, 14t, 14b, 16t, 17b, 18, 19b, 25b, 26t, 26b, 34.
NASA: Lick Observatory: 30t.
National Archives and Records Administration: 23.
National Oceanic and Atmospheric Administration: 38t.
Nature Picture Library: David Shale: 38b.
Photolibrary: Imagesource Imagesource: 30b, 47, North Wind Pictures: 35b, Frances Andrijich: 37b, North Wind Pictures: 10l, North Wind Pictures: 12, John Short: 13b, Mary Evans Picture Library: 16b, The Print Collector: 19t, Nativestock Pictures: 24b, Jeff Schultz: 27b, Jim and Mary Whitmer: 137b, Patrick Strattner: 146t.
Press Information Bureau: 45t.
Shutterstock: Robert: 28l, Luciano Mortula: 28r, Hugo Maes: 29t, Chee-Onn Leong: 31, Steve Estvanik: 32t, Bryan Busovicki: 32b, Caitlin Mirra: 33l, Cloki: 37t, Kevin D. Oliver: 40t, Donald R. Swartz: 40b, Scott Rothstein: 41t, Maksym Gorpenyuk: 41b, Denis Pepin: 42t, Domen Colja: 43t, Andesign: 5t, Quintanilla: 5b, Dmitry Rukhlenko: 6, Mg: 7, Jurand: 8b, Stocksnapp: 9t, T-Design: 10r, Cardaf: 21, Konovalikov Andrey: 27t.
U.S. Army Photo: 20.
Q2AMedia Art Bank: 36.

CONTENTS & QUESTIONS

Here's a look at some of the questions inside.

Why were the ancient Romans so powerful?

Ancient Rome was one of the mightiest civilizations on the planet. From about 31 B.C. to 476 A.D., Rome controlled most of the known world, including much of Europe, the Balkans, and the Mediterranean region. Rome became so powerful because its mighty army conquered these lands.

What were Roman families like?

Roman families included parents, children, and slaves. Generally, the father ruled the household. The average Roman family had five or six kids. Wealthy Roman families sent their children to school, while those with less money did not. In most households, boys and girls worked long hours in the fields.

Julius Caesar created a "newspaper" to let everyone know what Rome's leaders were doing.

WHO WAS JULIUS CAESAR?

Julius Caesar was a Roman politician and general who helped to transform Rome into the center of a great empire. He reformed Roman society and was proclaimed "dictator in perpetuity [forever]." A group of Roman senators, led by Marcus Junius Brutus, killed Caesar in 44 B.C., hoping to restore the Roman republic.

What destroyed the ancient city of Pompeii?

On August 24, A.D. 79, an eerie darkness covered the Italian countryside when Vesuvius, a 4,200-foot-high (1,280.16 m) volcano, blew its top. Soon, boiling mud and lava poured down the side of the mountain, burning everything in its path. Thousands in the nearby cities of Pompeii and Herculaneum raced to the sea to escape fiery death. Thousands more could not outrun the ash and lava. The city was destroyed.

WHY ARE SOME PEOPLE STILL AFRAID OF VESUVIUS?

Over the centuries, Mount Vesuvius has erupted with tremendous force, and many people are still afraid it will blow again. The next eruption could have serious consequences. About 600,000 people live in 18 towns in the so-called *zona rossa*, or red zone, close to Vesuvius. Scientists say during the first 15 minutes of an eruption, anything within a 4 mile (6.44 km) radius could be destroyed, including many towns in the red zone.

The dead of Pompeii are preserved forever in volcanic rock.

WHY IS THE ANCIENT CITY OF POMPEII SO WELL PRESERVED?

When Vesuvius was done spitting lava and ash on that awful day in A.D. 79, the eruption had buried Pompeii and other cities under a blanket of ash and mud, preserving them forever. Scientists encased the remains of some of those caught in the eruption in concrete after molds of the bodies were left in the hardening ash and mud.

Why did the Maya build pyramids?

Deep within the jungles of Mexico and Central America, the Maya, a Native American civilization, built amazing pyramids. The Maya began building pyramids mostly for religious purposes some 3,000 years ago. Some pyramids had stairs so people could climb to the top and hold sacrificial **rituals**. The Maya built the pyramids taller than the surrounding jungle so people could use them as landmarks. The Maya also used some pyramids as tombs for important government officials.

Some Mayan pyramids are as tall as a 20-story building.

WHY WAS ONE MAYA BALL GAME DEADLY SERIOUS?

In many countries, baseball is the ballgame of choice for millions of fans and players. In Mayan society, the ball-game wasn't as much fun—at least not for the losers. It gave new meaning to the baseball phrase "*You're outta here!*" The Maya used a rubber ball to play the game on a stone court. The goal of the game was to pass the ball and get it through a ring without having to touch the ball with your hands. The winners were treated as heroes and given a great feast. The losers were put to death.

WHY DID THE MAYAN CIVILIZATION DISAPPEAR?

For 1,200 years, Mayan society dominated life in Mexico and Central America. Mayan cities were crammed with people. Then the Mayan civilization disappeared. NASA scientists say drought and **deforestation** may have caused the Mayan civilization to collapse. The Maya destroyed their land to make a living in hard times. They cut down the jungle to grow corn to feed their ever-growing population. They also cut trees for firewood and for building homes.

Why did the Trojan War start?

The Trojan War is one of the greatest events in Greek **mythology** and is the inspiration for such epic Greek poems as the *Iliad* and the *Odyssey* of Homer. According to legend, the war began following the kidnapping of Helen of Sparta by Paris, the prince of Troy. Sparta was a **city-state** in ancient Greece. Helen's husband, Menelaus (men-uh-LAY-us), was the king of Sparta. He went to war with Troy to get his wife back.

Two residents of Troy argued against accepting the Trojan horse as a gift.

HOW DID ZEUS BECOME KING OF THE GREEK GODS?

In Greek mythology, Zeus is the king of gods and the ruler of Mount Olympus, home of the gods. Zeus is also the god of sky and thunder. Zeus became the supreme god by overthrowing his father. He then drew straws with his brothers, Poseidon and Hades, to see who would rule the world. Zeus won.

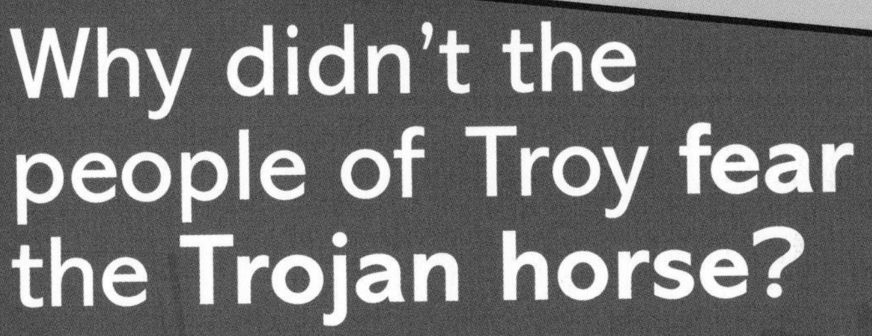

Why didn't the people of Troy fear the Trojan horse?

During the Trojan War, which is part of Greek mythology (in other words it may not have happened), Troy, a city located in modern-day Turkey, was pitted against the ancient Greeks. According to the myth, after a 10-year **siege** of Troy, the Greeks built a huge wooden horse. Several Greek warriors crept inside the horse and hid. As the Greeks pretended to leave, the Trojans pulled the horse into their walled city, believing it was a victory trophy. No such luck. The hidden warriors crept out of the horse at night, opened the front gates, and let the rest of the Greek army in. They destroyed Troy and won the war.

Where did the Vikings go in North America?

The Vikings of Scandinavia set foot in the New World 500 years before Columbus arrived. It was Leif Erikson who was the first Europeans to land in America. Around the year 1002, he set sail from Greenland and reached what is today Baffin Island in Canada, west of Greenland. He then sailed on to Labrador and into the Gulf of Saint. Lawrence. He built a settlement at L'Anse aux Meadows, Newfoundland, which served as a base camp for future Viking exploration of North America. The Vikings traded with the native population. Eventually the natives became unfriendly and the Vikings returned to Greenland but continued to sail to Canada for timber.

The Vikings arrived in America long before Columbus.

WHY DID SOME CONSIDER THE VIKINGS BARBARIANS?

Although some Vikings of Scandinavia had no problems raiding towns and villages along the coasts of Britain and France ("viking" is Scandinavian for "pirate"), most Vikings were peaceful traders, artisans, craftspeople, and merchants. The Vikings developed a complex farming society and a wide-ranging trade network in Eastern Europe that brought goods from as far away as the Orient. Vikings got their reputation as barbarians because Viking men would often join groups on voyages of plunder, attacking seaside towns and taking what they wanted.

Did Vikings really have horns on their helmets?

Although football's Minnesota Vikings have painted horns on their helmets, the real Vikings of Scandinavia did not wear horned helmets. Many ancient cultures wore horned helmets for ceremonies, but the helmets had fallen out of fashion by the time of the Vikings. If you see a painting of Vikings with horns on their helmets, you know the artist made a mistake.

Why did the Crusades begin?

Led by kings and knights, Christian warriors marched into the Middle East in an attempt to capture the "Holy Land" near Jerusalem from Muslim rulers. Those invasions were known as the Crusades. The First Crusade began in 1095. A highly trained force, including 4,000 knights on horseback and 25,000 foot soldiers, moved east in 1096. There were a total of eight crusades. The last one started in 1270.

WHY WERE KNIGHTS IMPORTANT IN MEDIEVAL EUROPE?

During the Middle Ages (5th to 16th centuries) in Europe, it was everyone's duty to obey the king. Landowners were the most powerful people. Kings gave their friends, known as noblemen, land for their loyalty. In turn, the noblemen relied on armed warriors, known as knights, to help them in battle and protect their land.

WHY DID PEOPLE BUILD CASTLES?

During the first part of the Middle Ages, people generally built homes out of straw, mud, and stone. Some even built small churches, but not much else. By A.D. 1000, people in Europe started erecting impressive churches. The Europeans also built castles out of giant stones for protection from attacking armies. Many medieval castles had towers and **spires**, steeply pitched roofs, and magnificent archways. Building a castle was time-consuming and difficult.

Why is the printing press one of the **most important inventions of all time?**

You probably think your iPod, iPhone, and your laptop are the most important inventions in the history of the world. Think again! Most people say the invention of the printing press was way more important. Prior to the mid-1400s, there was only one way to print a book—by hand. It was a long, hard, and expensive process. Only a few books existed, and only rich people could afford them. That all changed when Johannes Gutenberg, a German inventor, invented the printing press in 1440. The press made it easier to print books, and more people learned to read.

Before he was a printer, Johannes Gutenberg was a goldsmith.

WHAT WAS THE FIRST BOOK GUTENBERG PRINTED?

The first book to roll off the Gutenberg printing press was the Bible. No one knows how many Gutenberg printed, but some guess he produced at least 180 volumes. Some of Gutenberg's Bibles still exist today.

How did the printing **press help change world history?**

The printing press made it possible for individuals to read the ideas of other people. It also provided a way to share news and information. Some religious and political leaders feared such information and ideas would threaten their hold on power. They were right. The ideas of philosophers, priests, politicians, and others gained a wide audience around the world because of the printing press.
In many cases, those ideas started revolutions, as some people tried to change the way they lived and the way their governments worked.

Was the 100 Years' War really 100 years long?

From 1337 until 1453, the French and English fought what historians call the Hundred Years' War. Although historians are off by 16 years, the war started in May 1337, when France's King Philip VI tried to capture English territory in southwestern France. Of course, the English did not like this. Over the next 116 years, both sides fought, with brief periods of uneasy peace. The war ended when the French forced the English from the European continent.

Longbows were highly accurate weapons.

Medieval knights faded away at the end of the Hundred Years' War.

WHAT IS A LONGBOW?

The longbow played an important role throughout the Hundred Years' War. It was used mainly by the English and it was more accurate than the crossbows the French used. Some historians say a trained archer using a longbow could shoot 12 arrows a minute. Others say skilled archers could fire 24 arrows in 60 seconds. The arrows from a longbow could kill a soldier at 100 yards (91.4 m) and wound a soldier who was standing 250 yards (228.60 m) away.

WHY WAS THE HUNDRED YEARS' WAR A TURNING POINT?

The war marked the last time the English would try to control territory on the continent of Europe.

Why did Christopher Columbus **sail to**

?

If Christopher Columbus had a GPS system, he might not have reached the Americas. Instead, he would have made it to Asia. When Columbus sailed across the Atlantic in 1492, no one in Europe knew a New World existed. Columbus was looking for a short route to Asia. At the time, ships traveled around the tip of Africa to get to the Orient. When Columbus arrived in the Americas, he first believed he was in Asia.

WHY DID EUROPEAN EXPLORERS CAUSE PROBLEMS IN THE NEW WORLD?

Columbus opened the door for Europeans to come westward. Once the Europeans saw the New World, they began looking for gold and other treasures. They did not find gold, but the Europeans began exploiting the natives. They made slaves of the native people and took their land. The Europeans also brought weeds, rats, and diseases, which killed millions of natives.

WHY WAS CHRISTOPHER COLUMBUS ARRESTED?

Christopher Columbus first landed in Hispaniola, where he left some of his crew to set up a colony. When he returned in 1493, he found the colony in confusion. He tried to restore order. Many colonists went back to Spain and complained about how he ran the colony. A royal governor then came to America and arrested Columbus. When Columbus returned to Spain, the king and queen spared him from going to prison.

What was the Industrial Revolution?

The Industrial Revolution changed how products were made (in factories instead of at home). The Industrial Revolution began in England in the mid-1700s mainly because England had a wealthy economy that made it possible for businessmen to build factories. England was also home to brilliant scientists, which led to great inventions that helped factories make products.

Machines helped launch the Industrial Revolution.

Today's factories are much bigger than those of the Industrial Revolution.

WHY WERE MACHINES IMPORTANT TO THE INDUSTRIAL REVOLUTION?

Machines were the engines that drove the Industrial Revolution. Machines allowed factories to make goods faster and cheaper. The steam engine, for example, replaced the water wheel as a source of power. New devices, such as the carding machine, which turned wool into yarn, replaced old-style tools such as the spinning wheel and handloom.

Were George Washington's teeth really made from wood?

There are many myths surrounding George Washington's teeth. While it's true that Washington had several sets of false teeth, none were made of wood. His dentures were fashioned from gold, hippopotamus ivory, lead, and human and animal teeth. Washington's dentures had springs that helped them to open and bolts to hold them together.

George Washington had several pairs of false teeth.

DID GEORGE WASHINGTON REALLY CHOP DOWN A CHERRY TREE?

Like the wooden teeth myth, there seems to be no truth to the story that George Washington chopped down a cherry tree or that he confessed to his father, "I cannot tell a lie." The story was made up by a man named Mason Weems shortly after Washington's death. Weems made up the story to show how honest the "Father of Our Country" was.

Washington's slaves toiled at his home in Mount Vernon, Virginia.

WHY DID GEORGE WASHINGTON OWN SLAVES?

George Washington was a slaveholding farmer from Virginia. Washington inherited 10 slaves from his father. Eventually, he owned more than 300 slaves, who lived at Mount Vernon, his home in Virginia. Washington's slaves worked the fields and in his home, but when he died, they were freed.

Why did the American Revolution begin in Massachusetts?

For more than a decade, tensions between Great Britain and the American colonies ran high. The British had passed a series of laws to increase their control over the colonies. Colonists protested these laws, particularly in Massachusetts. To punish the colony, the British refused to let Massachusetts rule itself. Instead, the king sent royal governors to run the colony. In 1775, Britain declared Massachusetts (particularly Boston) to be in rebellion. The British sent troops to put down the "revolt."

WHERE WAS PAUL REVERE GOING ON HIS MIDNIGHT RIDE?

On the night of April 18, 1775, Paul Revere made one of the most famous trips in American history. An American patriot named Dr. Joseph Warren asked Revere to ride to Lexington to warn John Hancock and Samuel Adams that the British were about to arrest them. After Revere crossed the Charles River by boat, he waited for a signal to see which route the British were taking. Two lanterns hanging in the bell-tower of Christ Church meant that the British would row across the Charles River. One lantern meant they would march out of Boston. When two lanterns appeared, Revere borrowed a horse and hurried off. He was not alone that night. William Dawes and Dr. Samuel Prescott took a different route. Both warned the countryside that the British were on the move.

WHY DID AMERICAN COLONISTS WANT TO BREAK FREE FROM BRITISH RULE?

In 1763, the French and Indian War had come to an end. The cost of the war was huge. Britain forced the American colonies to pay for it. Tensions between the British king and the Americans grew as taxes and government rules were forced on them. By 1775, American colonists were growing more unhappy with British rulings toward the colonies. Eventually, the two sides clashed in battle, and the American Revolution began.

What is Charles Darwin's theory of evolution?

When Charles Darwin published his book *The Origin of Species* in 1859, it sent shock waves around the world. In the book, Darwin outlined his theories of natural selection and **evolution**. According to Darwin, plants and animals, including humans, changed over time. He said that organisms inherit new characteristics that allow them to survive and reproduce, a process known as natural selection. Darwin said that all living things came from a single common ancestor.

Charles Darwin first wanted to be a clergyman.

Why did Charles Darwin sail the world?

In 1831, Darwin set sail on the HMS *Beagle* as an unpaid **botanist**. The ship was on a British scientific expedition. In South America, Darwin found fossils of animals that were extinct, but resembled modern species. In the Galapagos Islands, in the Pacific Ocean, Darwin found many plants and animals of the same species that had different characteristics. These and other observations led Darwin to his theories about how life evolved over millions of years.

The HMS *Beagle*

WHY DID DARWIN WAIT YEARS BEFORE PUBLISHING *THE ORIGIN OF SPECIES?*

Upon his return to London, Darwin secretly worked on his theory. He said evolutionary change required millions of years. It took years before he published *The Origin of Species*. Darwin waited to make public his findings because he knew the book would create a controversy. Many scientists who were also members of the Church of England were critical of Darwin's theories because he challenged the Biblical version of Creation. Most scientists agree that Darwin's theories about how life on Earth evolved continue to hold up today.

Slaves used the Underground Railroad in all kinds of weather.

What was the Underground Railroad?

The Underground Railroad wasn't a real railroad. It was a system that allowed escaping slaves from the South to travel to the North to be free, especially during the 1850s and '60s. The slaves followed routes called "lines." People who helped the slaves along the lines were called "conductors." Houses along the way where slaves hid were "stations." The slaves themselves were called "packages."

Why did escaping slaves go to Canada?

The number of slaves escaping to freedom angered many Southerners. After the U.S. Congress passed the Fugitive Slave Act in 1850, it became illegal to keep escaped slaves in Northern states. So, escaping slaves had to travel to Canada, a foreign country, to be free.

WHY WAS HARRIET TUBMAN AN IMPORTANT CONDUCTOR ON THE UNDERGROUND RAILROAD?

Harriet Tubman was a slave in Maryland when she escaped from her owner and fled North to freedom. Later, she helped many people escape slavery. For 10 years, Tubman traveled to the slave-holding South to lead escaping slaves north to freedom. She later became a leader in the movement to free all slaves.

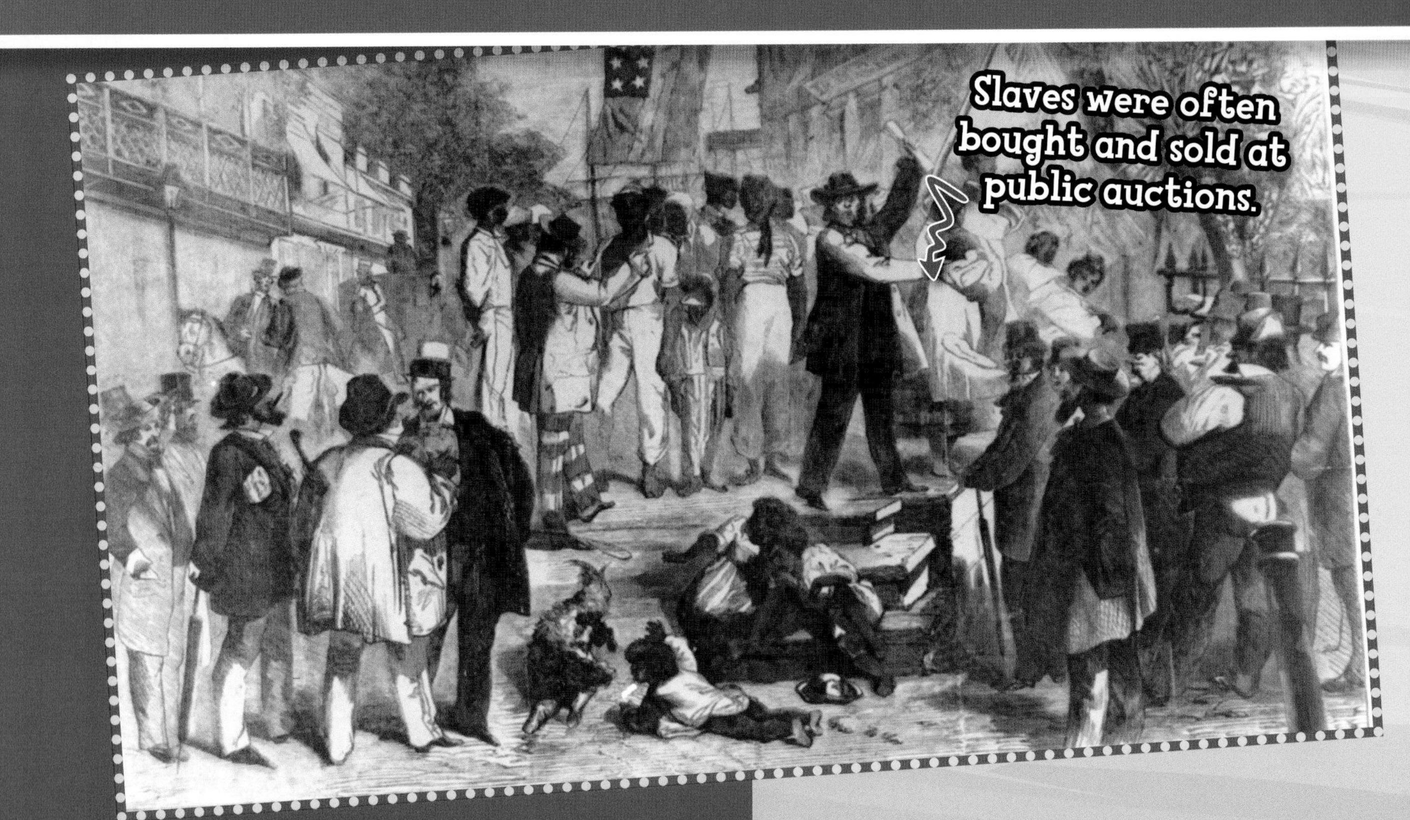

Why did Americans buy and sell slaves?

Long before the United States was the United States, slaves from Africa toiled on southern plantations and in the homes and ports of northern cities. The first slaves came to America in 1619, when a Dutch ship brought 20 enslaved Africans to the Virginia colony of Jamestown. Slaves were a cheap source of labor. They worked on sugar, rice, and cotton plantations. They also worked in homes in the North. Slavery became important in keeping America's economy growing.

Eventually, 4 million slaves were brought to America.

Why was the Civil War fought?

The issue of slavery was the chief reason the nation was split during the Civil War (1861–1865). Southern lawmakers wanted slavery to expand as America grew. The South feared President Abraham Lincoln would abolish slavery so it decided to **secede**, or leave, the Union. Lincoln had to keep the Union together. The Civil War began. By 1863, the war's focus changed from reuniting a divided nation to freeing the slaves.

Why did the *Titanic* sink?

The passenger ship *Titanic* was on its first voyage on April 14, 1912. The luxury liner hit an iceberg 380 miles (611.55 km) southeast of Newfoundland, Canada. The iceberg tore a huge hole into the side of the ship, which began filling with water. The ship broke in half and sank more than 2 miles (3.22 km) to the bottom of the North Atlantic.

Poor construction materials doomed the Titanic.

Why did the *Titanic* sink so fast?

Scientists say the *Titanic* sank so quickly because tiny metal fasteners called rivets that held the ship together didn't work the way they were supposed to. Scientists examined a few of the ship's rivets, which they brought up from the depths of the Atlantic. They found the metal fasteners were of such poor quality that they easily broke. When the *Titanic* hit the iceberg, the heads of the rivets broke off, popping the fasteners from their holes and opening up a huge hole in the ship. If the *Titanic*'s builders had used better materials, the ship would have stayed afloat longer, allowing more time for rescue ships to arrive.

WHY DID SO MANY PEOPLE DIE WHEN THE *TITANIC* SANK?

The *Titanic*'s engineers believed the ship was unsinkable, so they didn't provide enough lifeboats for all passengers and crew. The ship had only 20 lifeboats, which could carry about half of the 2,200 people on board. Only 705 people survived the sinking.

What war was called the "War to End All Wars"?

When World War I (1914–1918) began, no one imagined how brutal it would become. Soldiers used new weapons, such as the tank, poison gas, and the machine gun, for the first time. When the war ended, more than 40 million people had died. The war was so bloody and so devastating that many believed it would be the last war humans would ever fight—"The War to End all Wars."

Why did the United States enter World War I?

By 1917, most Americans sided with the British and French, who were fighting the Germans in World War I. Americans were angry because German submarines, or U-boats, were sinking American ships suspected of aiding Britain and France. In 1915, the Germans sank a passenger liner, killing 128 Americans. The Germans stopped the U-boat attacks for a while, but began the attacks again in 1917. On April 6, 1917, the U.S. Congress declared war on Germany.

American troops in World War I were part of the American Expeditionary Force (AEF).

WHAT NICKNAME DID AMERICAN SOLDIERS HAVE IN WORLD WAR I?

"Doughboy" was a slang term for a U.S. soldier in World War I. Many suspect the term was used in the Mexican-American War (1846–1848). American soldiers marching across Mexico, were often covered with chalky dust making them look like unbaked dough. Others think the term began in the 1840s and 1850s, when soldiers baked a dough-like mixture in their campfires.

What was the Cold War?

The Cold War wasn't a war fought with weapons. It was a war of ideas and competition between two systems of government: democracies and communism. The two nations most involved in the Cold War were the Soviet Union (Russia) and the U.S. When World War II ended, the U.S. wanted to stop communists from taking over other countries. The two nations made military treaties with other nations. Each side tried to gain superiority in space, sports, and weapons. The Cold War ended with the fall of the Soviet Union in 1991.

For years, only the Soviet Union and the United States had nuclear missiles.

What was the Iron Curtain?

In 1946, Winston Churchill, who led Great Britain during World War II, coined the term "Iron Curtain" to describe communist influence in Eastern Europe. In a speech to American students at Westminster College in Missouri, Churchill said an "iron curtain" had descended across Europe. On one side of that curtain, Churchill said, communist governments ruled with an iron fist. Throughout the Cold War, Churchill's Iron Curtain symbolized the differences between communism and the western democracies. It also symbolized the physical boundary that divided Europe at the time.

WHAT WAS THE BERLIN WALL?

The Berlin Wall divided West Berlin and East Berlin during much of the Cold War. After World War II, Berlin and Germany were divided. The Soviet Union and its allies controlled East Germany and East Berlin. The United States and its allies controlled West Germany and West Berlin. On August 13, 1961, the East German government built a wall to stop those living in East Berlin from escaping to the West. On November 9, 1989, the Berlin Wall came down when communism began to lose its influence in Eastern Europe.

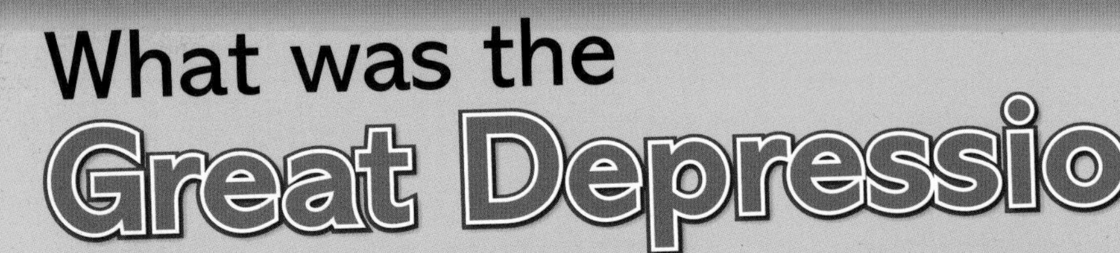

What was the Great Depression?

Soup lines were common during the Great Depression.

The 1930s were a terrible time in the United States. On October 27, 1929, the stock market crashed, sparking the Great Depression, the biggest economic disaster in U.S. history. Banks closed, factories went out of business, and people closed their stores. Farmers could not pay their mortgages, and people lost their homes. People lost their jobs and had little money to spend on the things they needed. When Franklin Roosevelt became president in 1933, about one out of every eight Americans was out of work.

WHY DID FRANKLIN ROOSEVELT USE A WHEELCHAIR?

When Franklin Roosevelt was 39 years old, he became ill with what was believed to be polio. He became unable to walk. Although he spent the rest of his life in a wheelchair, he did not let the disease ruin his life. He became governor of New York and, later, president of the United States.

When did the Great Depression end?

The Great Depression lasted about 10 years. When Franklin Roosevelt became president, he started programs to create jobs and slow the economic problems the Depression had caused. Roosevelt pushed through Congress his New Deal legislation. America became a welfare state—a nation that looks after the economic and social well-being of its citizens. The New Deal created 42 new government agencies designed to create jobs, control banks, and provide money to people out of work. These actions, plus the beginning of World War II, which enabled millions to find work in factories, slowly brought an end to the Great Depression.

Why did the Japanese bomb Pearl Harbor?

By the end of 1941, Japan had expanded its influence in South Asia. It had invaded French Indochina earlier in the year. In response, the United States cut off oil supplies to Japan. As Japanese and U.S. officials tried to work out a peaceful solution, the Japanese military came up with a secret plan to destroy the U.S. Navy fleet based in Pearl Harbor, Hawaii. The attack occurred on December 7, 1941. The next day, the United States declared war on Japan.

More than 2,000 people died at Pearl Harbor.

WHY DID THE U.S. DROP ATOMIC BOMBS ON JAPAN?

World War II ended in Europe in April 1945. The U.S. and its allies could then focus on winning the war against Japan. President Harry Truman ordered two atomic bombs to be dropped on the island nation, hoping this would force the Japanese to surrender. The first bomb exploded over Hiroshima on August 6, 1945. Three days later, another bomb exploded on Nagasaki. The Japanese surrendered on August 15.

WHY DO KIDS SEND PAPER CRANES TO JAPAN?

Each year, kids from around the world send paper cranes as a sign of peace to the Children's Monument in Hiroshima's Peace Park. The cranes were inspired by the story of Sadako Sasaki, who was two when the bomb was dropped on Hiroshima. The radiation made her sick and she died of leukemia in 1955. While in the hospital, she began folding cranes, believing that if she folded 1,000 she would be granted one wish. She only folded 644 before her death, but her friends folded the other 356 for her.

Why were some military codes in World War II spoken in Navajo?

The Japanese were experts at breaking secret U.S. military codes used for sending messages. A Marine named Philip Johnston, who knew how to speak Navajo, had an idea to use the Navajo language to send messages. Only a few people outside the Navajo nation knew the language. The Navajos who sent and translated messages were called code talkers.

WHY COULDN'T THE JAPANESE BREAK THE NAVAJO CODE?

The Japanese weren't even aware the Navajo language existed. Although the Japanese could hear the messages, they could not crack the code. To keep the Japanese guessing, the code talkers used three Navajo terms for most English letters. For example, "moasi" (Cat), "tia-gin" (Coal), and "bas-goshi" (Cow), all stood for the letter C.

HOW DID NAVAJOS COMMUNICATE WITH EACH OTHER DURING THE WAR?

To send a coded message, the Navajos strung together words in their own language. Code talkers receiving the message changed each Navajo word into English. They used only the first letter of the English word to spell out the code when they received the message.

Japanese internment camps in the U.S. were located mostly in the West and Southwest.

WHY DID THE U.S. FORCE JAPANESE AMERICANS TO MOVE TO PRISON-LIKE CAMPS DURING WORLD WAR II?

After the Japanese bombed Pearl Harbor, there was fear on the West Coast that Japanese Americans would act as spies. Following the attack, President Franklin Roosevelt signed an order allowing the U.S. military to move people of Japanese ancestry to internment camps where they were guarded at all times. About 120,000 Japanese, 70,000 of whom were U.S. citizens, were sent against their will to these prisons.

Were any Japanese Americans arrested for spying during World War II?

No. In fact, the government created an all-Japanese American military unit to fight in Europe. The unit received many awards and medals.

WHEN DID THE U.S. APOLOGIZE FOR THE JAPANESE CAMPS?

In 1988, Congress passed, and President Ronald Reagan signed, a law apologizing for the camps. He said the decision to lock up the Japanese Americans was based on "race, prejudice, war hysteria, and the failure of political leadership." It was the end to a sad chapter in U.S. history.

Nathan Hale was one of George Washington's spies.

WHO SAID "I REGRET THAT I HAVE BUT ONE LIFE TO LOSE FOR MY COUNTRY"?

Nathan Hale, one of America's most famous spies, uttered that phrase just before the British executed him during the American Revolution. George Washington had asked him to spy on the British in New York City. Writings have described Hale as a spy who couldn't keep quiet. Hale made friends with a man who Hale didn't know was a British spy. He invited Hale to dinner. where Hale talked about his mission. British soldiers arrested Hale and hanged him the next morning.

What does "Four score and seven years ago" mean?

"Four score and seven years ago" was the beginning of Abraham Lincoln's Gettysburg Address. It was a way to say how many years it had been since the Declaration of Independence was signed. A score equals 20 years. Four score equals 80 years. Add seven more years and the total is 87. Lincoln was in Gettysburg, Pennsylvania, in November 1863 (87 years after 1776), when he gave the Gettysburg Address.

The Gettysburg Address was only 267 words long.

Why do languages spread from place to place?

People speak English not only in the United States, but in England, India, and other countries. Portuguese is not just spoken in Portugal, but also in Brazil. French is spoken in France and in Quebec, Canada. There are about 6,800 languages around the globe. Languages have a shared system of sounds, words, and sentences that people can use to communicate thoughts, ideas, and emotions. There are many reasons why languages spread from country-to-country. The chief reason is that as people move, they carry their language with them.

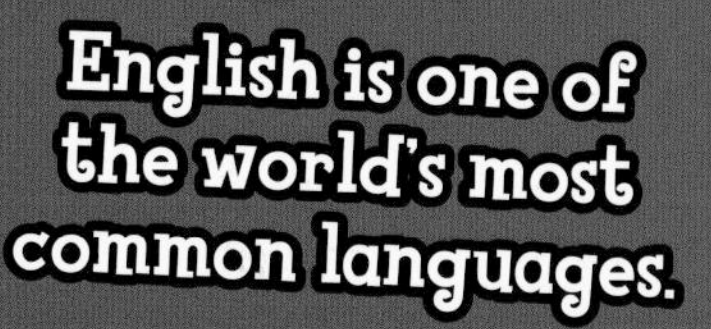

English is one of the world's most common languages.

WHY IS ENGLISH THE OFFICIAL LANGUAGE IN SO MANY COUNTRIES?

English developed in... where else? England! English spread throughout the world because England controlled a great empire during the 18th, 19th, and early 20th centuries. People in nations that were once part of the British Empire continue to speak English. Today, there are about 350 million people who speak English as their first language.

Why are some languages disappearing?

Experts say that half of the world's languages will be dead by 2050. Some say that 90 percent of languages could be extinct by 2100. Languages die when they are not passed to the next generation. For example, school children in Alaska are learning only two out of 20 native Alaskan languages. The other 18 languages are in danger of disappearing.

Why is the London Bridge in Arizona?

The famed London Bridge was rebuilt in Arizona.

The old nursery rhyme goes like this: "London Bridge is falling down, falling down, falling down..." In the late 1960s, that's exactly what was happening. Built in 1831, the London Bridge spanned the Thames River in London, England. By the late 1960s, the bridge was in disrepair, sinking under its own weight into the clay of the Thames. That's when Robert McCulloch bought the bridge for $2.4 million. In 1967, he moved the bridge brick-by-brick to Lake Havasu City, Arizona. By 1971, London Bridge was once again opened—this time in the U.S.

WHY IS VENICE SINKING?

For centuries, flooding has been a problem for those living in Venice, Italy, a series of islands in the Adriatic Sea. During high tides, water spills over the city's seawalls, flooding the city even more. Between 1950 and 1970, Venice sank 5 inches (12.70 cm) because engineers pumped water from under the city for use in factories on Italy's mainland. The pumping caused the seabed and buildings to sink. Venice continues to sink today.

WHY IS THE TOWER OF PISA LEANING?

Long before workers completed the third floor of the Tower of Pisa, the marble structure began tilting. The problem started when engineer Bonanno Pisano designed the 185-foot-tall (56.39 m) tower with a stone foundation that was only 10 feet (3.05 m) thick. The construction site was also very soft. Between the weak foundation and soft soil, the 16,000-ton (14.515 MT) structure tilted. To make up for this, the builders made each new floor a bit taller on the side closest to the ground. That made the tower lean in the other direction. Recently, engineers worked on the tower to give its unusual structure greater strength.

Why is an area in Beijing, China, called the **Forbidden City?**

Located in the middle of Beijing, China, the Forbidden City was once the imperial palace of Ming Dynasty rulers. For more than 500 years, the city, built between 1406 and 1420, served as the emperor's home and the political and ceremonial center of the country. The area, with its 800 buildings, was called the Forbidden City because only China's royal family could live there. Today, the Forbidden City is a popular tourist spot.

WHY ARE SO MANY PRODUCTS MADE IN CHINA?

From sneakers to toys, China makes just about every kind of product. In fact, China is the world's largest economy. The country manufactures and ships goods all over the world. One reason: The Chinese don't pay their workers much money. This makes it possible to produce cheaper (but not always superior) goods.

People are no longer forbidden in China's Forbidden City.

Astronauts really can see the Great Wall of China from outer space!

Can you see the Great Wall of China from outer space?

When astronauts orbit Earth they can see the Great Wall of China, but they generally need a powerful telescope. Built about 2,500 years ago, the Great Wall of China is 4,163 miles (6,700 km) long. NASA scientists say the Great Wall is often hard to see and photograph because its color blends in with the surrounding area.

Why did the Chinese build the Great Wall?

The Great Wall of China is actually a series of separate walls in the northern part of the country that the Chinese eventually linked. They built the wall to defend against attacks. An army of peasants, soldiers, slaves, and prisoners built the Great Wall. The wall stretches from Bo Hai Bay, on the eastern coast, to Gansu Province, in the western desert.

HOW LONG DID IT TAKE TO BUILD THE GREAT WALL OF CHINA?

It took several hundred years to build the Great Wall of China. The first section of the Great Wall was built in the 7th century B.C. In 221 B.C., the first emperor of the Qin Dynasty ordered that all the walls be joined. The Chinese built much of the wall by pounding earth between board frames.

What is the Chunnel?

Not long ago, the only way people could travel between France and England was by boat or by airplane. The two countries are separated by a body of water called the English Channel. In 1994, workers finished building a rail tunnel—nicknamed the Chunnel (a combination of "Channel" and "tunnel")—under the Channel, connecting the two countries. The 31-mile (50-km) tunnel makes traveling between the two countries easier as travelers ride a high-speed passenger train.

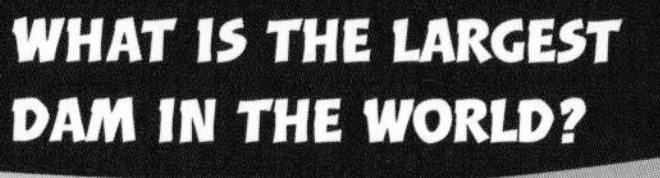

WHAT IS THE LARGEST DAM IN THE WORLD?

At 7,575 feet (2,309 m), the Three Gorges Dam in China is the largest dam in the world. The Three Gorges Dam spans the Yangtze River, holding back enough water to create a huge lake nearly 410 miles (660 km) long. Much like Hoover Dam in the U.S., the Three Gorges Dam generates electricity.

WHY DOES THE GOLDEN GATE BRIDGE SWAY IN THE WIND?

The bridge across San Francisco Bay in California was built to withstand earthquakes and high winds. When builder Joseph Strauss designed the bridge's center span (the distance between the bridge towers), he made sure the roadway swayed just a bit so the bridge would not collapse when the wind blew or the Earth shook. The Golden Gate Bridge can swing sideways up to 27 feet (8.23 m).

Why is the Statue of Liberty green?

The Statue of Liberty, which stands in New York Harbor, has always been a little green around the gills. The outer layer of the statue is made of copper. The copper reacts with wind, saltwater from the ocean, and other element,s including acid rain, to produce copper salts. The salts give Lady Liberty her greenish tinge.

WHY DID THE FRENCH GIVE THE STATUE OF LIBERTY TO THE U.S.?

At 151 feet (46.02 m), the Statue of Liberty is the tallest woman in the world. The French gave the statue to the people of America as a sign of friendship, which the two nations forged during the American Revolution (1775–1783). The statue is a universal symbol of freedom and democracy. French sculptor Frederic-Auguste Bartholdi was asked to design the statue, which was dedicated on October 28, 1886, and restored in 1986.

You have to climb 154 steps to get to the head of the Statue of Liberty.

Why is the Statue of Liberty holding a torch?

The original name of the Statue of Liberty is Liberty Enlightening the World. Frederic-Auguste Bartholdi designed the statue with a torch raised high in her right hand. The torch stands for the promise of America as a light of hope for the world. The torch also allows the Statue of Liberty to be used as a lighthouse.

WHAT WAS THE FIRST CAPITAL OF THE UNITED STATES?

The government called New York City its home from 1785 to 1790. The capital then moved to Philadelphia. By 1790, the U.S. Congress was looking for a permanent home. Members of Congress from the North and South argued over where that home should be. Finally, lawmakers settled on a plot of swampy land on the northern bank of the Potomac River that George Washington helped choose. Can you guess that city's name?

Why is the White House called the White House?

Long before the White House was the White House, it was called the President's House, the President's Mansion, or the Executive Mansion. According to legend, the White House got its name in 1811 when a coat of white paint was applied to its exterior. However, it was President Theodore Roosevelt who officially called the mansion the White House in 1901, when he had the name printed on his stationery.

It cost $23,796.82 in the 1860s to sculpt the Statue of Freedom.

What statue is on top of the U.S. Capitol?

The U.S. Capitol in Washington, D.C., is home to the U.S. Congress. Gracing the top of the Capitol's majestic dome is the bronze Statue of Freedom. The statue was designed by Thomas Crawford. The Statue of Freedom is a woman holding the shield of the United States with 13 stripes to celebrate the original 13 colonies.

Why didn't **George Washington** live in the White House?

Although George Washington helped pick the spot where the White House, or Executive Mansion, would be built, he never lived at that famous address. By the time the White House was completed, he had retired from the presidency. The cornerstone of the house was laid on October 13, 1792. Eight years later, President John Adams moved into the house. At the time, the building's paint and plaster were still drying. When Abigail Adams, the president's wife, arrived, she had to hang the laundry in what would become known as the East Room. Adams and his wife did not live long at that address, however. Thomas Jefferson was the second president to live in the White House, moving to the mansion in 1801.

Why was the **White House built by slaves?**

Slaves helped build the White House and the U.S. Capitol. Slave labor was cheap. The builders did not have to pay slaves. At the time, slavery in the South was legal. In addition, there were many slaves in Washington, D.C., because the city was a center for the southern slave trade. Many of the builders brought their own personal slaves with them to work on the job. They also contracted with plantation owners around the city to use their slaves.

WHY DID DOLLEY MADISON SAVE A PORTRAIT OF GEORGE WASHINGTON FROM A FIRE?

In 1814, Great Britain and the United States were still fighting the War of 1812. In August 1814, the British army was marching toward Washington. On August 24, the Americans lost a battle with the British a few miles from the capital city. With Washington, D.C., the next target, Dolley Madison, the wife of President James Madison, fled the White House by carriage, taking a full-length portrait of George Washington with her because Washington was an important figure in the new nation's history. That evening, the British marched into the city and set many buildings, including the White House, on fire.

Dolley Madison

Why are some deserts increasing in size?

Every year, on every continent, deserts are increasing in size—a process known as desertification. Bad farming techniques, the overgrazing of grassland by livestock, the destruction of forests by humans, droughts, and the overuse of soil all contribute to desertification. Researchers estimate that the expanding deserts affect some 200 million people living mostly in Africa, India, and South America. This has caused millions to leave their homes and lose their livelihoods.

WHY DOES FARMING CAUSE DESERTS TO FORM IN SOME PLACES?

People who farm in areas where the soil is poor and the climate dry often destroy native grasses and plants when they plow fields for crops. They also cut down trees so cattle and other livestock can graze. With no plants or trees to anchor the soil, wind and rain can wipe away topsoil, causing deserts to form.

WHAT IS THE LARGEST DESERT IN THE UNITED STATES?

Centered in Nevada, the Great Basin Desert is the largest desert in the U.S. It stretches into parts of California, Oregon, Idaho, and Utah. The desert covers about 190,000 square miles (305,775.36 sq. km).

Why does the South American country of Bolivia have two capitals?

What's the capital of Bolivia? If you said La Paz, you'd be right. If you said Sucre, you would be right, too. When Bolivia gained its independence from Spain in 1825, Sucre became the new nation's capital. In 1899, Bolivia had a period of political problems and many wanted the country's capital moved to La Paz. Many others disagreed. Eventually Bolivian politicians reached a compromise. La Paz became the seat of the **executive** and **legislative** branches of government, while Sucre remained home to the **judicial** branch.

Why is Easter Island called

The island, located in the Pacific Ocean about 2,300 miles (3,701 km) off the coast of Chile, got its name because a Dutch admiral landed there on Easter Day in 1722. Can you guess why Christmas Island in Australia is called Christmas Island?

WHY DO BRAZILIANS SPEAK PORTUGUESE INSTEAD OF SPANISH?

Although most of South America was colonized by the Spanish, the Portuguese colonized Brazil in the 1500s. At the time, most Brazilians spoke a language called Tupi. The Portuguese banned Tupi in the mid-1700s. Brazilians who speak Portuguese have mixed many Tupi words into their language.

Why do people call Australia the Land Down Under?

G'day, Mate! Welcome to the Land Down Under! Many people refer to Australia as the Land Down Under because it is one of only two continents located entirely south of the equator. Can you guess what the other continent is?

No part of Australia is more than 621 miles (1,000 km) from the ocean.

Was Australia really a prison?

Yes, Australia was founded as a giant prison, also known as a penal colony. In 1788, England sent its first shipload of prisoners to Australia to ease overcrowding in British prisons. The first ships of convicts landed at Botany Bay in New South Wales. Two more convict fleets reached the continent in 1790 and 1791. Although the first prisoners settled in Botany Bay, by the early 1800s convicts had settled in other locations. The prisoners worked as brick makers, carpenters, nurses, and farmers.

Australia's first aboriginal settlers came from Indonesia.

WHO ARE ABORIGINES?

Aborigines are native Australians whose ancestors migrated to the continent about 40,000 years ago. Each aborigine community has its own culture, customs, and language, much like Native Americans.

What is the deepest point on Earth?

The deepest site on the planet is the Mariana Trench, which is 36,201 feet (11,033 m) deep. The trench is located in the Pacific Ocean near the Mariana Islands, southeast of Japan. The reason the trench is so deep has to do with **plate tectonics**. Earth's crust is made up of moving plates, floating on the molten magma of the mantle. As the magma rises through cracks in the crust, it pushes the pieces of crust apart. In some areas, the magma forces chunks of crust together. In other areas, the ocean's crust pushes beneath Earth's crust, creating deep trenches like the Mariana.

The Mariana Trench is the deepest point on Earth.

WHY CAN'T PEOPLE DIVE TO THE BOTTOM OF THE MARIANA TRENCH?

If you were to dive to the very bottom of the Mariana Trench, you would be squished like a bug. The pressure at the trench's deepest point is 8 tons (7,252 kg) per square inch.

Angler fish

DO FISH LIVE IN THE MARIANA TRENCH?

Humans might not be able to survive at the bottom of the Mariana Trench, but hundreds of species of fish can. Species such as the angler fish and "vent crabs" thrive in the deep waters of the trench. One mud sample taken by researchers found nearly 200 different microorganisms. Not only do many animals survive in the waters of the trench, but many live for more than 100 years.

Why is Niagara Falls so large?

Niagara Falls, which borders Ontario, Canada, and New York State, began to form some 13,000 years ago as huge ice sheets carved out the Great Lakes. As Earth warmed and the ice retreated northward, melting water began to flow through present-day Lake Erie, the Niagara River, Lake Ontario, and the St. Lawrence River. Over time, rushing water created the falls from the surrounding rock. Niagara Falls is actually two falls in one, the American Falls and the Canadian or Horseshoe Falls. The American Falls is 1,060 feet (323.09 m) wide and 176 feet (53.64 m) high. The Canadian Falls is 2,600 feet (792.48 m) wide and 167 feet (50.90 m) high.

HAS ANYONE EVER TRIED TO GO OVER NIAGARA FALLS?

Since 1901, daredevils have attempted the famous stunt of trying to ride over Niagara Falls in a barrel or some other container. Annie Taylor was the first to do it and survive to talk about it. Others have gone over the falls in ball-shaped canisters, a jet ski, and steel barrels. Some have also walked across parts of the Niagara River near the falls on tightropes. About 15 people have gone over the falls in some sort of equipment. Five have died.

Why doesn't **Niagara Falls** freeze in winter?

With 150,000 gallons of water going over the falls every second, it's nearly impossible for Niagara Falls or the Niagara River to freeze over. However, an ice bridge often forms at the base of the falls and over a part of the Niagara River below the falls.

Why do people call **Chicago the Windy City?**

There are many theories about why Chicago is nicknamed the Windy City. Some suspect it has to do with the "wind," or lots of talk, by the city's politicians or the people who bragged about rebuilding Chicago after a fire in 1871 destroyed much of the town. Others say its because of how much real wind the city gets. The *Chicago Tribune* newspaper first used the term during the early 1880s, as a way to promote the city as a summer resort with cooling breezes coming off Lake Michigan.

WHY IS NEW YORK CITY'S NICKNAME THE BIG APPLE?

There aren't that many apple trees in New York City, but there are many theories on how the city got its nickname, the Big Apple. Some say sportswriter John J. Fitzgerald coined the term in the 1920s on a trip to New Orleans. Fitzgerald heard stable hands call New York's horse racing scene "the big apple." Fitzgerald returned to New York and named his horse-racing column "Notes from Around the Big Apple." The name supposedly stuck. Another story says that jazz musicians called their paying gigs "apples." The biggest "apple" of them all was to play in a New York City nightclub.

HOW DID NEW ORLEANS GET THE NICKNAME "THE BIG EASY"?

Some people claim New Orleans got its nickname the Big Easy because musicians could easily make money there. Others say New Orleans became the Big Easy because it was easy to drink alcoholic beverages there during Prohibition (1920–1933)—a time when it was illegal to buy or sell alcohol.

More than 8 million people live in the Big Apple.

Why did the ancient Egyptians **build the Great Pyramid?**

It is probably the grandest ancient building in the world—the Great Pyramid of Giza. Built from more than 2 million limestone blocks ranging in weight from 2.5 tons (2,268 kg) to 9 tons (8,165 kg), the 4,500-year-old pyramid was built as a tomb for King Khufu. Inside the pyramids and other tombs, the ancient Egyptians placed gold, sculptures, furniture, and other treasure that the king might need in the afterlife. They built pyramids because the shape was considered sacred.

WHY DID THE EGYPTIANS MUMMIFY THE DEAD?

In ancient Egypt, the bodies of dead rulers were preserved in a process that turned their bodies into mummies. The Egyptians believed the dead needed their bodies for the trip to the afterlife, so they carefully prepared the bodies for the journey. They placed the body's organs in special jars. They also preserved certain animals and household pets to be buried alongside the human mummy.

HOW DID ANCIENT EGYPTIANS MUMMIFY THE DEAD?

Researchers today believe that, after removing the person's lungs, stomach, and intestines through a hole in the body, and removing the brain through the nose, priests used a special salt to dry out the body. They packed the skull with salt and plaster, removing the dead person's real eyes and replacing them with artificial ones. Then they wrapped the body in linen treated with a special solution.

The Great Sphinx of Giza is half man, half lion, and stands 66.34 feet (20.22 m) high.

Why does planting a tree help the environment?

Breathe in. Now exhale. Everyone can thank the world's trees for those deep breaths. Planting trees helps improve the quality of the air we breathe by cleaning the atmosphere of carbon dioxide. When trees breathe in carbon dioxide, they exhale oxygen, which humans and animals need to live.

WHY ARE HUMANS BLAMED FOR POLLUTION?

Every time people turn on lights, ride in cars, or fly in planes, they are contributing to air **pollution**. Air pollution is the result of harmful air-borne substances, such as smoke from factories and electric plants, that can damage the environment and the health of humans and animals. Pollutants come in two main forms: gases and **particulates**. Gases are created when we burn **fossil fuels**, such as oil, natural gas, and coal. Particulates are tiny solid particles that automobiles pump into the atmosphere.

WHAT IS ONE REASON RAINFORESTS ARE IN DANGER?

One of the worst **ecological** disasters is taking place as you read this. In the world's rainforests, located mostly in South America and Asia, humans are cutting down and burning trees that soak up the **greenhouse gas** carbon dioxide. Greenhouse gases trap heat close to Earth's surface. The result is global warming, an increase in Earth's temperature. According to the Rainforest Action Network, humans cut down an area of rainforest about the size of a football field every second. This is known as clear cutting. With fewer trees, there is more carbon dioxide in the atmosphere. Clear cutting also destroys the habitat of thousands of animals.

A football field-sized chunk of the rainforest is cut down every second!

Why did the French **build the Eiffel Tower?**

Looming over Paris, France, is the Eiffel Tower, built for the World's Fair in 1889. Designed and built by Gustave Eiffel, the tower rises 1,063 feet (324 m) above the City of Light, almost twice as high as the Washington Monument.

Workers used 60 tons (54.4 MT) of paint to paint the Eiffel Tower.

WHY IS THE PARTHENON AN OPTICAL ILLUSION?

The ancient Greeks built the temple on top of a hill in Athens almost 2,500 years ago, wanting it to look perfect. To accomplish that goal, the ancient engineers needed to correct an optical illusion by creating one of their own. When seen against the sky, a straight column looks as if it gets narrow in the middle. To correct this illusion, the Greeks designed each of the outside columns with a slight bend. All lean inward, creating a picture of symmetry and straightness. If you cut the building in half, one side of the Parthenon would look the same as the other side.

WHY DID PEOPLE WANT TO BUILD A CANAL IN PANAMA?

For centuries, ships had to travel around South America to get from the Atlantic Ocean to the Pacific Ocean and back. It was a dangerous and expensive journey. Many people wanted to build a canal through Panama to connect both oceans because Panama was such a narrow strip of land. The French were the first to try, but their attempt failed in 1889. The United States then took over the project. Construction began in 1904. The work was so hard that an estimated 25,000 people died during 10 years of construction. The total cost was $375 million.

Why do all countries have a flag?

Each of the world's nations, from the tiniest to the mightiest, has a flag. Flags represent a nation and its people. A flag shows that the people are proud of their country. Some colors represent more than a historical event. They represent qualities or characteristics of a nation.

WHICH COUNTRY HAS THE OLDEST NATIONAL ANTHEM IN THE WORLD?

The national anthem of the Netherlands is the oldest. The song, "Het Wilhelmus," was written in 1815, but was not officially adopted by the Dutch until 1932.

Crowns are often made with jewels.

Why do kings and queens wear crowns?

Beauty pageant winners aren't the only people who get to wear crowns. Kings and queens have been wearing crowns for centuries. They wear them as a symbol of power, wealth, and honor. Crowns are usually fashioned out of gold and jewels. No one knows when the first crown appeared.

Who was **Mohandas Gandhi?**

Mohandas Gandhi (GON-dhee) was a lawyer who fought for India's independence from Great Britain during the 1930s and 1940s. Gandhi and his followers protested in nonviolent ways. One of those ways was to stage hunger strikes. Gandhi's most famous hunger strike came in 1932, when the British put him in jail for protesting the British government's decision to divide up India's electoral system by **caste**. He fasted for six days, until the British reversed the decision. Gandhi's nonviolence inspired his people and millions worldwide. As India inched toward independence, Gandhi's influence grew. He used hunger strikes as a way to win concessions from the British.

HOW WERE SLAVES FREED DURING THE CIVIL WAR?

President Abraham Lincoln freed the slaves two years after the Civil War began. The Civil War, between the North and South, began in 1861. The South wanted to break from the Union because Southerners did not want to end slavery. In 1863, Lincoln issued the Emancipation Proclamation, which declared slaves in the southern states to be freed. The Emancipation Proclamation also opened the way for blacks to join the Union army and slavery to be abolished forever.

HOW DID MARTIN LUTHER KING, JR., INSPIRE SO MANY PEOPLE?

Much like Gandhi, Martin Luther King, Jr.,a Baptist minister, used nonviolence to fight for civil rights for African Americans. King and his followers marched, protested, and staged **sit-ins** throughout the South during the 1950s and '60s hoping to make life better for millions of Americans. In 1963, King delivered his famous "I Have a Dream" speech in front of thousands of people at the March on Washington. The march was credited with helping to pass the Civil Rights Act of 1964, which outlawed many forms of racial segregation.

Martin Luther King, Jr., entered college when he was 15.

Web sites

Animals
The Animal Planet's http://animal.discovery.com/ is neat. There are games, videos, and blogs.

Earth
Take a wonderful journey across the globe with this Web site from the Smithsonian Institution: http://www.mnh.si.edu/earth/main_frames.html.

Space
NASA's Web sites are out of this world. Check out http://solarsystem.nasa.gov/planets/index.cfm and learn more about our solar system. Click on a planet and discover amazing facts.

Humans
Go to http://kidshealth.org/kid/htbw/htbw_main_page.html and learn how the human body works.

People and Places
Explore the world on http://www.nationalgeographic.com/. This amazing Web site links to parts of the world many people don't know about. You can access news features, maps, and videos and learn about many different people and places. For the latest news about people and places, go to timeforkids.com.

History
If you're a history buff, go to http://www.history.com/. Click on "This Day in History" to find out what happened on any particular day. Learn about world leaders and play dozens of games.

Science
Read more about the world of science with National Geographic at http://science.nationalgeographic.com/science/.

Technology
If you're interested in some of the dumbest inventions ever produced, the editors of *Life* magazine have put them all together for you at http://www.life.com/image/3270485/in-gallery/25371.

Arts and Culture
If you're interested in the art of the Renaissance, http://www.renaissanceconnection.org/home.html is a wonderful place to learn about how Renaissance artists lived and worked.

Sports
Sports and kids go together like, well, sports and kids. Keep up with all the news of sports and play some games at http://www.sikids.com/.

Book List

Animals
National Geographic Encyclopedia of Animals by Karen McGhee & George McKay, PhD (National Geographic Society, 2006)

Earth
Smithsonian Earth by James F. Luhr (Dorling Kindersley Publishing, 2007)

Space
Smithsonian Atlas of Space Exploration by Roger D. Launius & Andrew K. Johnston (Smithsonian Institution, 2009)

Humans
Human Body: An Interactive Guide to the Inner Workings of the Body (Barron's Educational Series, 2008)

People and Places
History of the World: People, Places, and Ideas by Henry Billing (Steck-Vaughn Company, 2003)

History
Children's Encyclopedia of American History by David C. King (Smithsonian Institution, 2003)

Science
The Science Book: Everything You Need to Know About the World and How It Works by Marshall Brain (National Geographic, 2008)

Technology
Computers and Technology by Tara Koellhoffer, (Editor) & Emily Sohn (Forward) (Chelsea Clubhouse, 2006)

Arts and Culture
Performing Arts (Culture Encyclopedia) by Antony Mason (Mason Crest Publishers, 2002)

Sports
The Greatest Moments in Sports by Len Berman (Sourcebooks, 2009)

botanist a scientist who studies plants

caste any of four main social classes into which Hindu society is divided

city-state a self-governing area, such as those in ancient Greece, consisting of a city and surrounding land

deforestation the cutting down of huge stretches of forest

ecological relating to an organism's relationship with the environment

evolution the theory that various plants and animals change over time to a different and usually more complex or better form

executive the branch of government responsible for the enforcement of the laws passed by the legislative branch of government; in the United States, the president is head of the executive branch.

fossil fuels fuels, such as oil or coal, that are created by plant and animal matter over millions of years

greenhouse gas a gas, such as carbon dioxide, methane, or nitrous oxide, that contributes to global warming

judicial the branch of government, including courts and judges, responsible for interpreting laws passed by the legislative branch of government

legislative the branch of government that makes laws

mythology a group of myths or legends belonging to a particular culture

particulates small airborne particles

plate tectonics the theory that explains the moving, or drifting, of Earth's continents

pollination the transfer of individual pollen grains from the male part of a plant to the female part of the plant which makes fertilization possible

rituals habits or customs

secede to break away from, or leave

siege to surround a place in order to force a surrender

sit-in a type of demonstration during the civil rights movement in which protesters refused to leave a particular building or area

spires tall, narrow, pointed structures located on the tops of buildings or towers

INDEX